Merthyr Tydfil Public Libraries
Llyfrygelloedd Cyhoeddus Merthyr Tudful
Renew / adnewyddu:
Tel / *Ffon*: 01685 725258
Email / *Ebost*: library.services@merthyr.gov.uk
Catalogue / *Catalogau*: http://capitadiscovery.co.uk/merthyr/

ISBN: 978-1-84527-326-2

Cover design: Design Department of the Welsh Books Council

Published with the financial support of the
Welsh Books Council

Published by
Gwasg Carreg Gwalch, 12 Iard yr Orsaf, Llanrwst, Wales LL26 0EH
℡ 01492 642031   🖷 01492 641502
✆ llyfrau@carreg-gwalch.com
Internet: www.carreg-gwalch.com

Welsh Women

4

Gwenllian

Warrior Princess

Siân Lewis

Illustrated by Graham Howells

'Gwenllian!'

The messenger's shout echoed through the hall at Caeo, where Princess Gwenllian was playing at sword fights with her four-year-old son, Rhys. As Gwenllian turned round in alarm, the little boy saw his chance. He rushed forward and tweaked her tunic with his wooden sword.

'I'm the winner!' he crowed. 'I've beaten you, Mam. Mam!' He tugged at her hand.

But Gwenllian had eyes only for the grim-faced man who was hurrying towards them.

'What is it?' she asked in a low voice.

'It's the Normans,' the man said hoarsely. 'There's talk that they're gathering in large numbers at Cydweli castle. If so, they'll soon be marching this way.'

'I'll drive the Normans back!' cried Rhys, waving his sword. 'I'm not afraid. Come on, Mam!'

But Princess Gwenllian had let her own wooden sword fall from her hand. For her the time for playing was over. Soon she would be fighting for real, and leading an army into battle.

It was the year 1136. Seventy years earlier the Normans had come across the sea from Northern France, and invaded and conquered England. Little by little they had invaded Wales too. Now their castles loomed over the Welsh countryside.

Aberystwyth … Cardigan … Carmarthen … Pembroke …Cydweli. Those castles, and many others, stood on land that had once belonged to the kingdom of Deheubarth. Gwenllian's husband, Gruffudd ap Rhys, was prince of

Deheubarth. Most of his lands had been taken by the Normans. All he had left was a small area in the Tywi valley.

Ever since he was a young man, Gruffudd ap Rhys had fought the Normans. He'd attacked their castles time and time again. But the enemy had strong walls to protect them. They were also well-equipped and well-trained. However hard he tried, Gruffudd was no closer to regaining his territory.

Then in early January 1136 the tide turned. Barely a month after the death of Henry I, the Norman king of England, a Welsh army won a victory at Llwchwr near Swansea. In the battle 500 Normans were killed.

After the battle, there was great joy and celebration in Gruffudd and Gwenllian's home at Caeo.

'At last!' said Gruffudd, rubbing his hands. 'The Normans are on the run. We must make sure they keep on running. I'll get an army together.'

'Then go north,' urged Gwenllian. 'Go to the court of Aberffraw, and ask my father and brothers for help. With their men as well as your own you can defeat the Normans once for all and drive them from Deheubarth.'

'Hm!' A frown crossed Gruffudd's face. Gwenllian's father was Gruffudd ap Cynan, the powerful king of Gwynedd. Gruffudd ap Cynan had fought many campaigns against the Normans. He'd even been a prisoner in Chester castle for twelve years. But he was an old man now, and rather too keen on peace and quiet for Gruffudd's liking. In fact he had once tried to hand Gruffudd over to the enemy to stop him fighting.

'You're thinking of that time when my father tried to

betray you,' said Gwenllian, shrugging impatiently. 'That was before you and I ran away together. Times have changed.' While Gruffudd still hesitated, she took his arm. 'My brothers, Owain and Cadwaladr, will be just as keen as you are to fight. Especially if they've heard of the victory at Llwchwr.'

Gruffudd nodded slowly. 'Yes, you're right,' he said. 'I'll head north to your father's house. But only after I've made sure that the Normans aren't up to any tricks.' His eyes lit up, and he squeezed Gwenllian's hand. Together they would defeat the enemy. They must!

That very afternoon, as the cold winds blew over Caeo, Gruffudd ap Rhys sent spies to keep watch on the Normans. Day after day he and Gwenllian expected to hear news of a Norman army on the march. But days turned into weeks, and still none came.

'The Normans are sheltering in their castles like squirrels in a drey,' said Gruffudd one morning. 'They don't like this cold weather.'

'Then go north as soon as possible before spring comes,' urged Gwenllian. 'Why wait?'

'I don't like leaving you here with no one to defend you,' said Gruffudd.

'No one to defend her?' interrupted a haughty voice. 'Who says there is no one to defend her? I am here to defend my mother.'

Gwenllian smiled. Striding towards her was Maredudd, her eldest son. He was only six years of age, but already had his father's fiery looks and his mother's determination.

'I can fight well, can't I, Mam?' he said.

'You can fight very well,' replied Gwenllian. It was true. Maredudd was already a fine little swordsman. It was she who had taught him to fight, just as her father had taught her when she was a girl in Gwynedd. 'See? You leave me in good hands,' she said to Gruffudd with a twinkle in her eye. 'Our son is a true descendant of the princes of Gwynedd and Deheubarth.'

'And I shall fight the Norman, till all that belonged to those princes is ours again,' said Maredudd, clasping the hilt of his small sword.

Gruffudd rested his hand on his son's shoulder. 'I'm sure you will,' he said. To his wife he murmured, 'But pray God you do not have to fight too soon. I may be gone some weeks.'

'The sooner you go, the sooner you will return,' replied Gwenllian stoutly. 'And the sooner you will defeat the enemy.'

A smile touched Gruffudd's lips. Gwenllian hardly needed anyone to defend her. Many a time she had fought by his side in the hills and the mountains. She was a princess by birth, the wife of a prince and the mother of princes. She was bold, strong, defiant, and also to his eyes the most beautiful woman in the whole of Wales. Her red-gold hair fell about her shoulders in a river of flame.

'Then go I shall,' he said, bowing before her and kissing her hand.

The very next morning Gruffudd saddled his horse, and with a small army of men to accompany him, he set off for Gwynedd. It was a bright February day. The animals' breath rose in a glittering banner on the frosty air, and sparks flew from their hoofs. Maredudd and Rhys ran after the horses for a short distance. Then, shouting 'God speed', they returned to their mother who was standing on the courtyard with Morgan and Maelgwn, their two baby brothers, in her arms. Surrounded by her four boys Gwenllian listened till the sound of hoofbeats had died away. Only then did a shadow of anxiety cross her face.

The Normans were cunning. Would they know that Gruffudd had gone, and that she had been left with few men to defend her? She turned and gazed across the wooded slopes of the Tywi valley. Apart from a band of rooks chasing a solitary buzzard, all was peaceful.

'Gwenllian!'

It was early morning on the last day of February, when the peace was shattered and the messenger brought Gwenllian the news that she most feared.

'Gwenllian!' She knew at once by the sound of his voice that the Normans were preparing for battle. In the still of the night, when she lay awake in her bed, she had already decided what to do if that should happen.

She would fight.

But first she must make sure that Maredudd and Rhys were safe. Small as they were, they'd be clamouring to join in the battle. Glancing at Rhys who was fighting his shadow, she called a maid. 'Find Maredudd,' she whispered to the girl, 'and take him and Rhys into the countryside out of the way.'

The maid took the little boy's hand and led him out. At

once Gwenllian turned to the messenger. 'Now tell me where the Normans are,' she urged. 'How far advanced are they?'

'They are still gathering in Cydweli castle.'

'Then we must attack without delay, otherwise our lands are lost,' said Gwenllian.

'But won't you wait till your husband returns?' the messenger asked anxiously.

'If we wait, we lose our lands,' Gwenllian replied. 'The Normans know that Gruffudd is away. That's why they have chosen to attack at this time. What they do not know is that I will take his place. Our only hope is to take them by surprise. I will lead the army.'

'You have hardly any men!'

'There are plenty of Welshmen who are willing to fight the Normans. Call them. Summon them. We shall march at once.'

The messenger left the hall in haste. Soon Gwenllian's call to arms was echoing over the Welsh countryside. From every corner of the Tywi valley, working men left their labours, shouldered their arms, and hurried to answer the call.

Amongst them was a young lad called Hywel Goch. He was in the woods hunting rabbits, when he heard the sound of the trumpet. He was thirteen and this would be his first taste of battle. But he did not hesitate. With a bow in his hand and a sword at his side, he joined the stream of men who were heading towards Caeo.

As they approached Gruffudd ap Rhys's home, Hywel heard a voice ring out above the heads of the crowd. It was the voice of Princess Gwenllian.

'Men of Deheubarth,' she cried. 'Will you join me in battle?'

'Yes!' The men roared their reply.

'I am the daughter of a king, but you are the sons of Wales. This land is yours and mine. The Normans have already stolen much of our birthright. Shall we let them steal even more?'

'Never!'

'Then we shall march this very day and defeat them!'

With a shout the men surged forward, taking Hywel with them. They passed a cart carrying two baby princes. Princess Gwenllian herself rode at the head of her army, her red hair whipping in the breeze. 'Death to the Normans!' she cried, and from hill and dale, men heard her cry and rallied to her side.

By afternoon Gwenllian's army numbered two hundred and more and was already within sight of Cydweli castle. But it was still early in the year, and the days were short. As the sun began slipping below the horizon, a man came running towards Gwenllian along the banks of the Gwendraeth Fach. It was the same messenger whom she had seen that morning, and his face was as grave and as fearful as before.

'My lady!' he cried. 'You are already too late. Maurice of London, Lord of Cydweli castle, has heard that you are coming. You can no longer take him by surprise. He's ready for you. He and his army have set up camp.'

Gwenllian reined her horse, and turned her head in the direction of Cydweli. Beneath the castle walls a last glimmer

of sunlight burned brightly and mockingly on the chain mail of the enemy soldiers. She thought of her own men in their rough working clothes. Should she retreat?

No! She looked about her. Her men might be poorly clad, but no one could match the pride that burned in their eyes. Even her two tiny sons, Morgan and Maelgwn, seemed to be urging her on. There could be no turning back now.

'Tonight we shall camp here in the shadow of Mynydd y Garreg,' Gwenllian announced, 'but tomorrow we shall fight for what is truly ours.'

'We shall fight!' With one voice the men shouted their defiance. They went on shouting till the rocks of Mynydd y Garreg resounded with their cries.

Next morning, on the first day of March at first light, Gwenllian was woken by the sound of tramping feet. She took a last look at her babies and snatched up her sword. The massed ranks of the Norman army were already on the move. Gwenllian's men gathered behind her and watched the Normans advance along the banks of the Gwendraeth Fach, their banners fluttering in the breeze. First came the archers with their bows and arrows, then the mighty cavalry.

'Gwenllian!' The call from the messenger was sharp and urgent. 'Look behind you. They are coming at us from two directions.'

'Then to battle, men of Deheubarth,' cried Gwenllian. 'With your backs to the hills, fight!' Tightening her grip on her sword, she raised it in the air.

With a roar her army turned in a half-circle to face the enemy. Her archers let loose their arrows. Her dagger men charged. A hail of enemy arrows drove them back. As men fell to the ground, the swordsmen ran forward with Hywel in their midst.

Still the Normans advanced. Whenever one fell, six more would take his place. Sword held high, Gwenllian spurred her horse and launched herself into the fray. Her men surged behind her. Before them they saw the faces of the enemy who had already taken their land and were hungry for more. Roaring their defiance, they set about them with dagger and sword, and hammer and spear.

Welshmen and Normans fell together. Still the hordes of the Normans came relentlessly on. As Hywel swung at the enemy, his sword was knocked from his hand. He fell to the ground and, as he scrambled for safety, he heard a frantic whinny. An arrow had struck Gwenllian's horse. The animal reared, and with a wild look in his eye, he unseated his rider and galloped towards the river.

'Gwenllian is down!' yelled Hywel in dismay. 'Help her, men! Help her!'

But there was no one to help. The Welshmen who were still on their feet were pinned against the rocks and fighting for their lives.

'Gwenllian is down!' Now triumphant Norman voices took up the cry, and across the battlefield towards the captive princess strode their leader, Maurice of London, Lord of Cydweli castle, with a savage smile on his face

Gwenllian lifted her proud head. 'Fight, men of Wales. Fight!' Her war cry echoed over the battlefield one last time.

Then all was silent.

That night, as he made his way back towards Caeo, Hywel wept for the loss of Gwenllian. Maurice of London had spared her no mercy. He had put her to death on the battlefield, along with one, if not both, of her baby sons. As he wept, his fellow-Welshmen wept too, and their plaintive cries of 'Gwenllian!' echoed through the dark countryside.

While the defeated army limped home, another band of Welshmen was preparing to march south from Gwynedd. At its head was Gruffudd ap Rhys, Gwenllian's husband, and her two brothers, Owain and Cadwaladr. Gruffudd's efforts to raise troops in the north had met with great success. His father-in-law, in particular, had been very welcoming. Now that he was an old man, over eighty years of age, Gruffudd ap Cynan liked to look back over his long life, and to talk about Gwenllian, the youngest of his eight children.

'You should have known her when she was a youngster,' he said to Gruffudd. 'She was afraid of nothing and could handle a sword or a bow better than her brothers. Yet she was as pretty as a sunbeam.'

'She's still the same,' smiled Gruffudd. 'And the sooner I get back to her the better.'

Some days later, on their way south, Gruffudd and his men camped in Merioneth. That night Gruffudd dreamt of Gwenllian. In his dream Gwenllian was galloping to meet him on a white horse with a golden sword in her hand. He was still rubbing the dream from his eyes, when the sound of a real horse made him sit up. Through the morning mists came a man riding hard and calling his name.

'Gruffudd ap Rhys! Gruffudd ap Rhys! I bring you news.'

'What?' Gruffudd leapt to his feet.

The rider thundered into the camp, and was soon surrounded by the men of Gwynedd.

'Gruffudd ap Rhys!' he cried. 'Where is Gruffudd ap Rhys?'

With a chill in his heart, Gruffudd approached him. 'Here I am,' he said.

'Sire!' His shoulders heaving, the rider dismounted and dropped on one knee.

'What is it?' asked Gruffudd.

'The Princess Gwenllian is dead…'

'Dead?' cried Gruffudd.

'She died in battle at the hands of Maurice of London,' said the rider, still trembling. 'As did your little son Morgan. And Maelgwn is lost.'

'Morgan and Maelgwn too!' Gruffudd buried his face in his hands.

'But we still hear her, sire,' said the rider plaintively. 'Gwenllian's ghost roams the battlefield without rest and urges us to fight, though there is no one to fight any more.'

'No one to fight?' choked Gruffudd. 'No one to fight? I shall fight to my last drop of blood.' With a roar of rage and grief he leapt on his horse and held his sword in the air. 'Gwenllian! Revenge for Gwenllian!'

'Gwenllian! Revenge for Gwenllian!' The cry was taken up, and as one man, the army rampaged southward. 'For Gwenllian! Revenge, revenge!' The cry echoed around the hilltops, making the Normans' blood run cold.

'Revenge for Gwenllian!' The furious Welshmen attacked the castles of north Ceredigion. They swept over the enemy in a torrent. Fires were lit and men burnt. As the Normans fled for their lives, they heard the Welshmen's victorious cry.

'Gwenllian! This is Gwenllian's revenge!'

Despite the determination of Gwenllian's husband and brothers, and despite their victory at Cardigan later that year, the battle between Welsh and Norman would rage for many generations, leaving thousands dead. Gruffudd ap Rhys himself died a year after his wife. Of their four sons, only Rhys survived to a ripe old age.

By the time he died, though no longer a prince, Rhys ap Gruffudd was the greatest Welsh lord of his time. He had learnt his lessons well at his mother's knee, and had become a powerful warrior. In Deheubarth he regained many of the lands his family had lost, and won others besides. At one time he was lord of Cydweli castle itself. Another of his castles was Cardigan, where in 1176 he founded the first Welsh eisteddfod.

At the eisteddfod poets and musicians came to sing the praises of Rhys himself and of the Welsh heroes and heroines of old. We shall never know the words of their poems and songs, but we can be sure of one thing. They would have sung to Lord Rhys of a woman, whose bravery no one had forgotten: Gwenllian.

Today the spot on the banks of the Gwendraeth Fach where she fought and died is still called Maes Gwenllian – Gwenllian's Field. Close by are the empty walls of Cydweli castle.

Dwynwen

The story of Dwynwen, a beautiful princess, whose father refused to let her marry the man she loved. So she left home, set sail on a boat, and let the wind blow her wherever it chose. Despite being unlucky in love, Dwynwen's dearest wish was for other lovers to be happy.

Marged

Marged was a tall, strong, extraordinarily talented woman, who would take no nonsense from anyone. But she did have a soft spot for her terrier, Ianto. Surely no one would dare to harm little Ianto? But someone did . . .